A

FEW

WORDS

Written By

Raymond Stewart
Aka
"Twilight"

your love
is plain
to see.

"Your Humble
Servant

Twilight "

The following pages are dedicated to

Tiffany D. Martin, my loving daughter

Tiffany is the world's greatest daughter. I know that all little girls love their dads, but my Babydoll's love for me is so clear that you can see it from miles away. It has been said that love is an action word that you can see. You not only can see her love for me, you can hear it in these few words I put on this paper. Can you hear it?

I have been away from my daughter since she was three years old; she is thirty-two now. I have seen her a few times a year and spoken with her on the phone. We even wrote each other letters when she was five or six years old. She has never forgotten to tell me she loves me when closing any conversation. I once told her, "One day I'll make you proud of me, Babydoll." She looked at me with those big, pretty eyes and says, "I am proud of you now, Daddy. You have always treated me good, and supported me in whatever I do. Mostly you have never told me I was wrong about anything. I love you, Daddy."

Yes, she is the world's greatest. She breaks my heart. I love you, Babydoll. Can you hear it?

Contents

Contents Continued

Contents Continued

Contents Continued

<u>ACKNOWLEDGEMENTS</u>

My parents: My father made me strong, my mother made me understanding.

My sister Brenda gives me commitment to family.

Annie Paskil gives me a Foundation.

Martha Champion makes me know we are all connected.

Pastor Scott makes me see grace.

Tiffany D. Martin makes me see true love.

Brenda Bean guides me through the wilderness.

Darryl Moore aids in my search for liberation.

Dova Webb brings me back to the illusion of life.

Kelly Shirley makes me know someone else loves humanity.

Karli Rutherford makes me realize I can control the beast within.

The Men of Journey, Amos, Karl, Jack, David, Tom, Banks, Frank and "The Rock" Hank give me a clear vision of a brighter tomorrow.

E.V.P., Rose, Craig and Alex have transformed me from the chaos effect to a part of a collective solution.

Dr. Kate King, through "Inside Out" and "The Think Tank," has empowered me more than words could describe. She is the catalyst of this book of Haiku and the reason I can see everyone else has value. She made me realize that I have value, as well, with something to add to the creation of a better tomorrow.

Hank and Nancy Miles for editing my book.

Photographs by Janice Denton.

Thanks to them all.

INTRODUCTION

A Few Words is a book of Haiku describing how my life has been enriched and my understanding enlarged through conversations with others. *A Few Words* will let you to see things differently than you ever have. It will take you from sanity to insanity, then leave you sane.

Through my desire and willingness to learn from others I was able to see that my mind was in pieces. My mother, my daughter, my grandchildren, my friends, my past, my present, my future, humanity, God, and my situation all had a piece of my mind. A few words with others have begun to bring my mind to wholeness.

I am not completely whole yet, but a few words have changed the pieces into a few chunks. I believe *A Few Words* will have a profound effect on your life.

To God be the glory!

<u>Connection</u>

A Dream I Must Share

Of Her Walk Through The Valley

Same Path I Once Walked

A Dream I Must Share

There are times when we have dreams of friends and family that we are not sure we should speak of. Then there are dreams that we must speak of. This is one of those dreams.

I dreamed that a friend was in a room filled with hat boxes, but in the boxes were dead bodies. I came to realize that she was surrounded by the spiritually dead. So I let her know of the dream.

A few months later I saw her in another dream. This time she was in a warehouse filled with hat boxes, and in the boxes were dead bodies. I came to realize that she was becoming more and more surrounded by the spiritually dead.

I prayed for her to change her surroundings because I didn't want to see her in a hat box.

Of Her Walk Through the Valley

When we share our thoughts and dreams with others, we only want to increase their boundary of understanding. We hope that this increase will aid them in their daily walk through the valley.

You see, the valley is deep, wide, and endless in length, with danger every thought of the way.

It is not physical danger, but spiritual danger, I am talking about. The valley is within, and your walk through it will determine if you will reside in a hat box or not.

So please, don't allow residents of the hat box world to choose your address.

<u>Same Path I Once Walked</u>

Her spirit is bright and growing brighter with each breath she takes. There are people within her circle that really don't like this bright spiritual growth.

You see, spiritual growth brings you out of darkness, but not everyone wants to come out of darkness. It is just too pleasing to them and they don't know why it no longer pleases her.

This is when the connection with the children of light and the children of darkness is broken. When you come to the realization that light and darkness cannot occupy the same space, you are almost home.

Inspired by Martha Champion

<u>Empty</u>

I Live In Your World

You Wish To Live In My World

Can They Coexist

Perfection

Looks Like Her Mother

Kindness Is Her Father's Gift

A Blessing To Me

<u>Clear Vision</u>

'Til My Mind Is Right

We Shall Walk in Darkness! Why?

No Light in My Mind

<u>'Til My Mind is Right</u>

We know that we are at war and it is being fought within our mind. Some think that the war is black against white, gang against gang, country against country, but this is far from the truth.

The war is good against evil or, more plainly put, right against wrong.

You decide which side wins the war, but by deciding the winner, you also decide the loser.

The war is for your life!

Consider that.

We Shall Walk in Darkness? Why?

I say WE because the ancient Egyptians believed that all time exists simultaneously: Past; Present; and Future. All the wrong I did in my past was me, and there is no defense for my wave of destruction; that was me.

All the right that I do now can in no way make up for the wrong I did in my past. I would never consider that; this is me.

What I do in the future, whether it is guided by right or wrong, will be me.

We all believe that the right thing is what we will do in any given situation. For certain, whatever I do will be me.

So I say WE because past, present, and future is all me. Consider that.

No Light in My Mind

Faith: confident belief in the truth, value, or trustworthiness of a person, idea, or thing.

Faith is the light that illuminates and destroys the darkness from my mind.

Faith is the force that makes the vision of my future so clear.

My vision is a brighter tomorrow that I will have the pleasure of helping bring to pass.

Consider that.

Inspired by
David, Banks, Jack, Tom, Karl, Frank, Hank, and Amos
The Men of Journey

<u>Conflict</u>

No One Protects Me

From The Enemy Within

His Goal? Destroy Me!

<u>Unworthy</u>

Forgiveness I Have

But My Past Still Cripples Me

My Shame Is So Great

Empowerment

Broken By Myself

Put Back Together By You

Forgiveness Keep Me

<u>Broken by Myself</u>

When I was a child, I was afraid of the dark. I was too young to know that darkness is only the absence of light. This same darkness that filled me with such fear, I became. You see, I confused darkness with bad, and fear with respect.

I felt that if I was bad enough, then people would respect me. But now I know that bad is a conscious decision: to be evil and wicked.

But darkness is not bad! It is only the absence of light.

Fear is alarm and agitation caused by the expectation or realization of danger.

Respect is earned by submission to another's opinion, wishes, or judgment.

Respect is looking to assist, simply because there is a need.

Consider that.

Put Back Together by You

There are people we meet in life that have the ability to disempower or empower you.

To be disempowered could cripple and paralyze you mentally for life. My disempowerment was done by myself, simply by lack of understanding.

There have been a lot of positive people, books, and songs that have empowered me. I had a professor from Western Kentucky University named Dr. Kate King, who taught Victimology, who had a profound effect on my life.

I was empowered so much that I was able to realize that my life was being lived in fear. You see, if anybody offended me in some way, whether it be physically, mentally, or verbally, I could not let them get away with the offense. I was so afraid that if I allowed one person, just one, to get away with offending me, then people would walk all over me forever. I was enabled to focus not on future offenses, but the positive possibilities that forgiveness will bring in the future.

Consider that.

Forgiveness Keep Me

Forgiveness: To excuse for a fault or offense.

You have heard so many times before that it is harder to forgive yourself than to forgive anybody else. I say forgiveness is an action word that can be seen by others.

You see, after you pray to the God of your understanding for forgiveness, your walk will change because you know that you have been excused for the fault.

We really cannot be surprised if people refuse to forgive us. We can only let them know that we realize we offended them, and ask forgiveness.

But we will pray to the God of our understanding for the power not to offend another.

Consider that.

Inspired by Dr. Kate King

<u>Hunger</u>

Could I Bite You Once

It Would Never Be Enough

I'll Thirst Forever

<u>Definition</u>

You Make Me Worthless

What You Think Was My Value

Love Gave me Self Worth

Foundation

Good Against Evil

Was Clear To All Who I Served

Thanks! My Eyes Opened

Good Against Evil

I was doing time at a prison in West Tennessee and I found myself in a physical confrontation with another prisoner.

When the confrontation was over, an officer by the name of Annie Paskil approached me and said, "You ain't nothing but the devil."

I was without a clue, and said to her, "I'm not the devil. What are you talking about?"

I was about to tell her how only the strong survive when she smiled and kindly explained to me that if we are not working for God, then we are working for the devil.

We can say what we want with our mouth, but our actions tell who we serve.

Was Clear to All Who I Served

A few months later, I found myself in another confrontation.

After I had put him down and was about to bash his head in, I could see Annie Paskil's words clearly. I could see the fear on his face. He was petrified. He had the look of doom, and hopelessness, as if he was looking at pure evil. ME!

It broke my heart because now I, too, could see the words she shared with me.

Thanks! My Eyes Opened

For a long time it bothered me, not being able to bash his head in. I felt like I had become weak.

While I was on lockdown, I began to read the Bible and grow in the Spirit. The more I read, the more I grew, and it pleased me.

One day I read Ecclesiastes 1:18. It said: "For in much wisdom is much grief: and he that increaseth knowledge increaseth sorrow."

It was Annie Paskil who increased my knowledge and created a foundation in me that is unbreakable. You see, it was the kind words of knowledge that she shared with me that opened my eyes. To have eyes and not be able to see the devil within, was scandalous and profound.

I never had a chance to say thanks, so thank you, Ms. Paskil. You gave me a foundation and saved me.

Inspired by Annie Paskil

Reflection

You Heard Of Goodness

At Times I Saw Pure Evil

Sometimes It Was Me

<u>Confused</u>

Who Am I? You Know

Not Who I Want To Be! Why?

Fear Has Held Me Back

True Love

Over And Over

It Has Been Asked, What Is Love?

Now It's Plain To See

Over And Over

People tell each other all the time, "I love you." My grandparents told one another, my father told my mother, my mother told my father. I've even told a few women, "I love you so very much," not really knowing the meaning of the words.

Some say it is just a cliché that has been used from the beginning of time.

Whatever the case, all mankind will use it sometime in their lives.

It Has Been Asked, What is Love?

We say it all the time, but it is really hard to put the definition into words. These are a few ways it has been described:

It makes me feel good just to be around you.

I care more about you than I care about myself.

The sight of you makes me so happy.

I can't imagine life without you. Just the thought of you is love.

It is the good feeling I have inside.

And most of all, it is the safe feeling I get when you look at me.

But there is really no description that do these words justice.

There is only one thing for sure, no description is an absolute.

Now It's Plain To See

The first sight of my daughter made my heart skip a beat. She was drop-dead gorgeous, and I knew who and what I wanted her to be. Within ten minutes of the first sight of my baby, I had planned her whole life. I loved her so much; I expected so much from her; if she would only do as I say, everything would be beautiful.

We know with expectation comes disappointment. To plan the lives of your children, or anyone, is called an unrealistic expectation.

The first sight of my first grandchild made it plain to me what love truly is. Within ten seconds of that first sight of my grandson, my heart danced. He made me happy just to meet him; he made me happy to be alive. Mostly I do not expect anything from him. I only want him to be happy.

If we could only see everybody in this same light, it would make the world a place full of true love.

Inspired by Tiffany D. Martin

<u>Warriors</u>

We Fight The Same Fight

Our Enemy Is Within

Always In The War

<u>Birth</u>

Fathers Say Bless Me

A Curse Is What God Called It

Mothers Say Thank God

<u>Transformed</u>

Think You're One Person

You Wish To Be Another

Unknown Who You Are

Think You're One Person

Society has a strange influence on how we define ourselves. You have to be careful of the definition you are getting of yourself from society.

It could be negative and destructive once this unhealthy definition of yourself brings you to the place where you think much too highly of yourself It is the beginning of your end.

It is brought on mostly by pride and the false self-portrait of yourself. The belittlement of others is the fuel of pride that makes you think you are better than others.

Be careful! The problem is, you might not be the person you think you are. Society just might see a different you.

You Wish To Be Another

Another: (core meaning) Distinctly different from the first.

There are times in our lives when we wish to be more, do more, and leave a mark on society. To be remembered forever would be a beautiful thing.

It has been said that when a person thinks like this, they are not happy with who they are. So it is safe to say that I am not happy with who I am, because I want to do great things.

I came to the realization that society is broken, and I wish to be the one to fix it. You see, I am the chaos effect, the bird that flapped his wings in China who started the brokenness that is being felt all around the world. All of the hurt, pain, and suffering that society endures is because of me.

Yes, I do wish to repair the brokenness of society.

Unknown Who You Are

In the summer of 2011, I had the pleasure of participating in a leadership and transformational thinking workshop called End Violence Workshop. E.V.P brought me to a point of wanting to know who I was through a series of introspective group discussions.

I say WAS because who I thought I was, I know now that I am not.

Through these life enriching discussions, I was brought to the realization that if I only fixed myself, that in actuality I would be fixing society. I know now that I love people, all people, and that everyone has value. I don't need to be remembered, I just need to be part of the solution for a collective of people to create a world that is safe, good, and real.

Real: (core meaning) The quality or state of being actual or true.

That is who I am, only a part of the collective solution.

Inspired by E.V.P. Rose, Craig, and Alex

<u>Alive</u>

Pleasing To My Eyes

You Belong To Another

A Rose I Won't Touch

<u>Enemy</u>

Your Mouth Says One Thing

Your Actions Show Another

Imposter You Are

Wilderness

I Knew I Fit In

Now That I Think Different

I Belong Nowhere

I Knew I Fit In

I not only walked through the valley of the shadow of death, I became the valley of the shadow of death.

We know that the wickedness that we face in everyday life is the valley of the shadow of death. That was my world, and the more wicked I became, the more people cheered.

For me, I liked for people to cheer for me. That was like saying, "We love you".

But their cheers were not for love, they were for the gladness that they were not the focus of my wickedness.

I was good at this life.

Now That I Think Different

Different: (core meaning) Not like another.

When I began to look at myself differently, I looked different. When I honestly looked inside myself and saw myself for who I really was, it broke my heart.

I saw the hate, anger, rage, pride, and vengefulness.

But what hurt most of all was what I didn't see: peace, respect, trust, understanding, or love.

To see the monster within is a scary thing, and with this fear comes a great responsibility.

I Belong Nowhere

There are times when someone will vex my spirit or upset me. It is in these times that I will go off by myself, be quiet, and just listen.

Sometimes I know that it is self-pity that is going on, and the self-pity noise is so loud that I cannot hear myself. It sounds something like this:

Who do they think they are?

They can't treat me like that.

They can't talk to me like that.

I can't allow them to do that.

I had a supervisor who made me realize that I was allowing their bad behavior to cause me to want to act badly. She said people think highly of you and see you as a man of God. When you cripple your testimony for God, it could hinder someone's growth in God.

You see, when it is all said and done, I belong to God in good times and bad times, in life and in death. My walk will reflect that.

Inspired by Brenda Bean

<u>Lost</u>

Made In God's Image

Followed The Ways Of Satan

Have Mercy On Me

__Hurt__

Your Words Are Not True

But They Still Destroy My Life

The Pain Is So Deep

<u>Liberation</u>

Say You Want Freedom

For Some It Could Be Scary

I Would Rather Serve

Say You Want Freedom

A large percent of people see freedom as physical only.

We get this perception at a young age, when we don't like the rules given to us by our parents. Here are some of the thoughts we first had within ourselves for physical freedom:

I can't wait to be grown. I'll do as I want.

I'll stay up all night.

I'll go where I want.

I won't allow anybody to tell me what to do. I won't ever be this hard on my kids.

If you do not realize that your parents are giving you rules and discipline to create a responsible individual, you could become enslaved by physical freedom.

<u>For Some It Could Be Scary</u>

We could not wait to become adults. We were certain it would give us freedom.

Now we wonder what is causing us so much fear.   Could it be that while we were in such a hurry to become adults, we left valuable lessons behind? Lessons like responsibility, self-discipline, self-respect, integrity, and most of all, the ability to deny our destructive nature.

You see, without character, we can become enslaved to greed, desire for wealth, drugs, alcohol, anger, and violence. The most frightening of all is that we know we have an addictive nature, so freedom is only an illusion for us.

Consider that!

I Would Rather Serve

I grew up in a family with nine children. We were dirt poor, but there was a lot of love in our house. I learned the value of self-discipline at a young age.

We lived next door to a church until our parents separated. Then I went astray. I will not say that is the reason that I became enslaved to wickedness and walked such a dark path, because I have successful siblings.

This is what I know for certain: that I have identity, it comes from my Father, and it is HE that I identify with. He loves humanity and wishes only to be a blessing to all. When I am able to be of service to others, it makes me feel good. I feel it down in my stomach. Joy! You see, with my freedom, I freely choose to be of service to others.

I am not well, but I am a better part of humanity than I was.

You have probably heard of my Father. He had a lot of good men write a book for us all.

It is called the Holy Bible.

Inspired by Darryl Moore

<u>Holistic</u>

Don't Have To Like You

But I Must Truly Love You

My Soul Is At Stake

74

<u>Future</u>

He Made Only One

But I Wish They Could Clone You

Could One Be For Me

__Illusion__

Wish To Enjoy Peace

Should Be Preparing For War

Trouble Comes Sudden

<u>Wish To Enjoy Peace</u>

Peace: (core meaning) The absence of war or other hostilities.

When I ask people to flash back to the time of their childhood and tell me what they wanted to be when they grew up, the majority of them wanted a career in which they would help others.

When I flash back to my childhood, I have come to the realization that I never wanted to grow up. You see, I saw the ugliness of the world that adults faced in everyday life, and it broke my heart at a young age. I felt that if I didn't have to deal with the ugliness of the world, that it might not be real.

This is the same illusion that many adults have today.

Should I tell them that peace is only a dream to be dreamed? It will never be obtained, for we know that war and hostilities are always present.

Should Be Preparing for War

Prepare: (core meaning) Pre= before, Pare= to get ready

Life is the time between birth and death. The war is between thinking and knowing. The war is taking place right now, and it is being fought within all of us.

The THINKER thinks birth is a blessing and death is uncertain.

The KNOWER knows that birth and death are both curses, and the only thing that is real is the way you spend the time you have between the two.

The THINKER thinks death should never come to their young loved ones.

The KNOWER knows that death belongs to us all, and longevity is not promised to any.

The THINKER thinks the pain of right now will be over soon, and tomorrow will be a better time. The KNOWER knows the pain will always be, and it will not get any easier, but you will get stronger. The KNOWER knows that tomorrow never comes, and all that is real is right now.

So prepare for the war, and it will not destroy you.

78

Trouble Comes Sudden

Sudden: (core meaning) Taking place without warning.

When pain and suffering comes to us without warning, it leaves us with a numb, helpless feeling that seems to linger. It is in this state of helplessness that we find ourselves asking the God of our understanding, "Why?" We want to know, "Why, God, did you let this happen, and if it had to happen, why, God, did you have to let them die? You save people all the time, God. Why, God? It's just not fair." These feelings are normal and they have pushed some to the point of no return.

I have a friend who lost her brother Donovan to a violent crime, just when he was getting his life together. The last conversation she had with him left her with great hope and expectations for him. When he was taken from her, it left her mad and angry with God. No one can really know the bond they shared. Her feelings are real, and no one has the right to tell her how to grieve. I had a short conversation with her on the phone, and I felt her pain. I told her that I could not fix her brokenness, so I would not try. I told her I would pray that her faith would not fail her, and when she was stronger, to help her family because they would need her to keep from being destroyed.

Inspired by Dova Webb

Deception

Thought I Was Good Man

My Foundation Was Broken

My Tongue Knew No Shame

Collective

Why Do You Think Small

Too Many Thoughts Of Others

Now We Think For All

<u>Family</u>

Oldest She Is Not

She Has Most Love For Siblings

Head Of Family

Oldest She Is Not

If you were to meet the siblings all together, you would swear she was the oldest. She has a look that makes you know she means what she says.

All the siblings fear her, even the oldest.

As I look back, I can clearly see she wants the best from us all, and wants us to do the right thing in any given situation.

For this, we fear her.

She Has Most Love For Siblings

Whenever a family member needs help, she is there.

If you need a soft bed to rest your body, she is there.

If you need a warm conversation to strengthen your mind, she is there.

Whatever the sibling needs, gladly she is there.

Head Of Family

It is not by birthright, and not because she is the oldest.

It is plain to see, she is the most committed to the well-being and survival of the family.

Inspired by Brenda Stewart Morrow

Future

A Message I'll Send

To Tell Of My Love For You

What Joy To Meet Her

<u>Vivid</u>

The Vision Is Mine

I Will Present It To You

A Bright Tomorrow

<u>Humanity</u>

Beat Down By Your Life

But You Continue To Stand

May I Stand With You

Beat Down By Your Life

You smile so brightly; you are beautiful, smart, and committed to whatever you do. But most important of all is your love for all people.

You carry the weight of the world on your shoulders. You feel responsible for us all, but because of your blank stare and the sadness in your eyes, it is clear to see the concerns of mankind have taken hold of you.

It is an unhealthy hold that is seeking to destroy you.

But You Continue To Stand

You wake every morning to fight the fight of helping all the ones in need, and the need is so great. I say fight because no one seems to care, and you are certain the fight is yours and yours alone.

Sometimes you wonder why so few people show compassion and love for others. You find yourself laying down at night and crying, trying to figure out why you stand and continue to fight.

May I Stand With You

I know why you stand. You stand because you love people. Most people think if you give to others it will leave you with less. This is not so.

You are a candle that has lit a thousand other candles. The light that shines through the thousand candles is because of you.

Most of all, your light is not less, but brighter and shining through a thousand others.

Your light is trust, hope, faith, compassion, and most of all, love for humanity.

I must admit my light is much brighter because of my interaction with you.

Keep up the fight and remember that I am on the battlefield beside you, and the fight is not yours alone, but ours.

Inspired by Kelly Shirley

<u>Complete</u>

I Was Born A Male

I Grew To Become A Man

Made Whole By My Mate

Krista

My Life! A Puzzle

I Cannot Put Together

Pieces Are Missing

Control

Lion I Was Born

A Wild Beast Became My Life

Meek I Pray To Be

Lion I Was Born

Lion: A person felt to resemble a lion, as in fierce and brave; a person of extraordinary importance or prestige, a king.

I was taught at a young age that I should not allow anyone to hit me and get away with it. If I couldn't beat them, I was to pick up something and bust their head to insure that they would never touch me again.

You see, self-preservation was key for me and mine.

A Wild Beast Became My Life

I became a wild animal, a very brutal person. I was under the impression that I had to conquer the strong and destroy the weak.

I felt like the means justified the end. The means was my knowledge of violence, and the end was my control of others.

I really cannot put into words where this impression came from. It is more than likely a combination of things. As I look back, I can clearly see I walked a wicked path, without shame for my actions.

May God forgive me.

Consider that.

<u>Meek I Pray To Be</u>

I had the pleasure of meeting a young lady who has the heart of a lion and the meekness of a lamb. She speaks boldly and respectfully to all. It is plain to see that fear does not dwell within her. She is humble and gentle; she is power under control.

I have heard of people who give you joy just being around them. This is who she is. She makes me realize that there is a choice in the middle of "fight or flight."

Consider that.

Inspired by Karli Rutherford

<u>Abused</u>

You Want Me To Trust

Deceptions Are All You Offer

Pain Still Has Me Down

Scandalous

You Beat Me So Bad

Tell Me Why I Still Love You

Family You Are.

Grace

Captive By Our Crime

But Our Death Will Release Us

Immortal By Faith

Captive By Our Crime

I say OUR because we are all connected. We are fathers, sons, nephews, brothers, uncles, enemies, and criminals.

But above all, we are children of God who have somehow lost our way.

We never dreamed of this life, but it is ours.

But Our Death Will Release Us

Some of our brothers knew that death was close at hand. It pushed some away from God, but pushed some closer to God.

I will not name names, because that just would not be right.

You see, some have already died to their criminal, dark life and moved into the light.

That is the lesson left to us by our brothers: to die to our criminal dark life and move into the light.

Consider that.

Immortal By Faith

Change means making something different, not better or worse. Change is neutral and can be either negative or positive.

Now I will give you a few words to help your change be an immortal change.

I COULD have been a lot of things. You CAN be a lot of things.

I am fifty-five years old now; my life is almost over. I have been in prison over thirty-four years in all. I took the easy ride, which led to a life of misery, not only for me, but for my loved ones as well. I am sure you can all take the easy ride and be tough guys and spend a lot of your life in prison, maybe even die in prison. But a change will make people care, love, and remember you. If people remember you, you become immortal.

"For God so loved the world, that he gave his only begotten Son, that whosoever believeth in him should not perish, but have everlasting life." (John 3:16)

Inspired by Pastor Scott

About the Author

I was born poor and raised in the hood. I am the youngest of four sons, and the eighth born of nine children. I am the one who could not imagine a world without me in it. Now I can't imagine a world without you in it. You are the most important person in my life; you represent light and goodness in a dark world. I am only the sum of conversations with you. I am empowered.

We all know the world is broken, but nobody wants to take responsibility for the brokenness. You made me realize it was broken by many, and it will take many to repair it. Most of all, you don't speak about the problem, you only speak of the solution.

Now that is a new conversation and I am open to the possibilities of it.

Thank you,
Twilight

Made in the USA
Columbia, SC
13 September 2017